Swahili
phrasebook

Robert Leonard

Swahili Phrasebook

Published by
  Lonely Planet Publications
  Head Office: PO Box 88, South Yarra, Victoria, 3141, Australia
  Also: PO Box 2001A, Berkeley, CA 94702,USA

Printed by
  Singapore National Printers Ltd, Singapore

First published
  March 1988

Editors	Mark Balla
	Susan Mitra
Design, cover design & illustrations	Greg Herriman
Typesetting	Ann Jeffree

National Library of Australia Cataloguing in Publication Data

Leonard, Robert
  Swahili Phrasebook

  ISBN 0 86442 025 0

  1. Swahili language – Conversation and phrase books – English. I. Title.
  (Series Language survival kit).

496.39283'421
© Copyright Lonely Planet, 1987

Contents

Introduction

The Swahili speaking peoples were urbanised and sophisticated centuries ago. Early on, they were extensive travellers and traders. They built stone towns in which multi-storied houses featured running water and drainage systems well before such features were at all widespread in Europe.

A useful attribute of the Swahili culture is its ability to incorporate outside influences and ideas. The grammar of Swahili is almost purely Bantu, and while its vocabulary is also largely Bantu there are also a significant number of borrowed words from Arabic – primarily religious and cultural words. Swahili has taken many words from English and other languages, in particular, words having to do with western technology and culture.

The Swahili language has become the most important indigenous language in East Africa and a major lingua franca of the African continent.

Swahili (or Kiswahili as it is called when one is speaking the language) is the national language of Kenya and the official language of Tanzania. It is spoken as a first language on the east coast of Africa and the islands adjacent to the coast, from southern Somalia in the north down through the Kenyan and Tanzanian coasts to approximately the border of Tanzania and Mozambique in the south.

It is also spoken as a second language by millions of people, mainly in Kenya, Tanzania, Uganda, and eastern Zaire. There are also speakers in Mozambique, Rwanda, Burundi, Zambia, Malawi, and even in southern Arabian countries such as Yemen and Oman.

While there are many different varieties of Swahili, for our purposes we can group them all into two divisions: coastal Swahili and upcountry Swahili. Schooling and migration has in many areas spread coastal Swahili into regions where historically one could only have heard upcountry Swahili.

Coastal Swahili is the native language of the Swahili people, who live mainly on the east coast of Africa. There are three major dialect areas: Lamu, Mombasa, and Zanzibar. For political and religious reasons, the colonials chose the Zanzibar dialect to be the basis for standard Swahili. Swahili has a several-hundred-year-old history of written poetry (almost entirely in the Lamu dialect). The past decades have also seen the publication of numerous novels and plays (almost all in standard Swahili).

Upcountry Swahili is spoken inland. It is the descendant of the trade language that arose when speakers of other languages wanted to communicate with Swahili speakers who in the last two centuries established inland trading centres. The reason a trade language comes into being is not for the expression of lofty sentiments, or the writing of religious poetry, but as the name implies, trade. What comes about is a language variety that has a reduced grammar and vocabulary. The hallmarks of such a language are that it is no one's native language and it is used only for trade or other limited activities.

Coastal Swahili is the variety used in this book and will be referred to simply as 'Swahili'. The small number of upcountry Swahili phrases are labelled as such.

In East Africa, the language of banking, immigration, airports, post office, and the like is English. This book therefore does not include sections on these topics.

A highly recommended resource is Madan & Johnson's *A Standard Swahili-English Dictionary* (Oxford University Press). Much more than a dictionary, its detailed explanation of the meanings of Swahili words provide an insight into the various cultures associated with the Swahili language.

Pronunciation

There are three golden rules for those wanting to learn Swahili.

Pronounce the Swahili words slowly. You will be much better understood.

Pronounce each Swahili syllable distinctly. Try to give each syllable just about equal weight.

Pronounce all vowels in full. In English, we reduce certain syllables. In Swahili we do not. Compare the first and second syllables of English 'mama' – the first has a full **a**, the second a 'reduced' vowel, an **uh**. Try to say both syllables with the full **a**. This is how it would be said in Swahili. In Swahili there are no reduced vowels. In English, no matter what the spelling suggests, vowels are often reduced to these **uh**-type vowels, for example the **a** in 'about', the **e** in 'kitten', the **er** in 'further'.

Swahili is rather easy to pronounce. Although several sounds are not pronounced the way their equivalents are in English, their English values will suffice.

The stress almost always falls on the second last syllable.

Vowels

	English			Swahili	
a	as in	'far'	*dada*	–	'sister'
e	as in	'may'	*wewe*	–	'you'
i	as in	'see'	*sisi*	–	'we'
o	as in	'old'	*toka*	–	'leave'
u	as in	'too'	*lulu*	–	'pearl'

One reason that English speakers have such distinctive accents when they speak foreign languages is that in English **e** and **i** are pronounced with a little **y** at the end, and **o** and **u** are pronounced with a little **w** at the end. Say the English words in the vowel table very slowly and you will hear and feel what we mean (the **w** is much easier to detect than the **y**). Swahili vowels are pure vowels, that is to say, they are the vowel part alone, without the **y** or **w** that we add in English. (In both English and Swahili, **a** is a pure vowel.)

Consonants

Some consonants that need explanation are:

	English		Swahili	
dh	as in	'this'	*dhambi*	– 'sin
th	as in	'thing'	*thelathini*	– 'thirty
ny	as in	Spanish: *señora*	*nyasi*	– 'grass
ng'	as in	'singing'	*ng'ombe*	– 'cow
gh		made in the same place in the mouth as 'g', but more like a gargle. If you can't do it, say 'g' instead.	*ghali*	– 'expensive'
r		the same as in Spanish or Italian. If you say 'd' instead you'll be very close. English 'r' will be understood	*sukari*	– sugar

Grammar

The grammar of Swahili, like that of any language, cannot be completely summarised in a few pages. Here, instead, is a short course in 'survival Swahili' that will teach you enough to let you begin constructing your own phrases.

Verbs

The basic Swahili verb is simpler than that of most European languages. Tenses are totally regular, and there are no lists of endings to memorise for each tense.

Information about the subject and the tense are tagged on to the verb in the following way:

	subject marker	tense marker	verb stem	
English	I	past	eat	– I ate
Swahili	*ni*	*li*	*kula*	– *nilikula*

To change the meaning, we plug in a different subject marker, tense marker, or verb stem in the same order as shown above.

These are the subject markers:

I	*ni*	we	*tu*
you	*u*	you plural	*m*
he/she	*a*	they	*wa*

This is how the different subject markers are plugged in:

	subject marker	tense marker	verb stem	
English	you	past	eat	– you ate'
Swahili	*u*	*li*	*kula*	– *ulikula*
English	they	past	eat	– they ate
Swahili	*wa*	*li*	*kula*	– *walikula*

Now to change the tense we need the following tense markers:

past	*li*
present	*na* or *a*
future	*ta*
perfect	*me*

	subject marker	tense marker	verb stem	
English	we	future	eat	– we will eat
Swahili	*tu*	*ta*	*kula*	– *tutakula*
English	I	future	eat	– I will eat
Swahili	*ni*	*ta*	*kula*	– *nitakula*

Notice that there are two tenses that mean 'present'. For our purposes we will treat them as identical. The only thing of note is that the *a* causes some sounds to combine and change, so instead of saying, *ni-a-taka*, 'I want', one says *nataka*. In meaning these two present tenses are the same:

	subject marker	tense marker	verb stem	
English	I	present	want	– I want
Swahili	*ni*	*a*	*taka*	– *nataka*
English	I	present	want	– I want
Swahili	*ni*	*na*	*taka*	– *ninataka*

Some common verb stems are:

want	*taka*
like, love	*penda*
go	*kwenda*
speak	*sema*
understand	*fahamu*
know	*jua*
come	*kuja*

We can plug these in as shown in the following example:

	subject marker	tense marker	verb stem	
English	I	future	want	– I will want
Swahili	*ni*	*ta*	*taka*	– *nitataka*

Negative Verbs

In English you make something negative by putting a negative word in front of a positive verb, like 'I eat', 'I don't eat'. In Swahili other things change.

The negative verb's structure is essentially the same as that of the positive verb, the difference being that we plug in negative subject markers and negative tense markers. The verb stems are the same.

These are the negative subject markers:

'negative I'	*si*
'negative you'	*hu*
'negative he/she'	*ha*
'negative we'	*hatu*
'negative you' (plural)	*ham*
'negative they'	*hawa*

Here are some negative tenses:

past	*ku*
present	*0-i*
future	*ta*
perfect	*ja*

Combining the negative prefixes with the verb stem gives the following result:

	subject marker	tense marker	verb stem
English	negative I	negative past	want – I didn't want
Swahili	*si*	*ku*	*taka* – sikutaka

The negative present needs some explanation. The 0-i means that there is no tense, and that the final vowel changes from *a* to *i*.

	subject marker	tense marker	verb stem
English	negative I	negative present	want – I don't want
Swahili	*si*	–	*tak-i* – sitaki

Objects
Objects follow the verb.

We eat meat.	*tunakula nyama*
We don't want meat.	*hatutaki nyama*

Independent Pronouns
These do not have to be attached to a verb, in the way a subject marker does. When there is a subject marker as well

as an independent pronoun, the independent pronoun gives more clarity but is not essential. Remember that an independent pronoun is never a substitute for a subject marker; if a construction requires a subject marker, it must be included whether or not there is an independent pronoun. The independent pronouns are:

I, me	*mimi*	we, us	*sisi*
you	*wewe*	you (plural)	*nyinyi*
he, him/she, her	*yeye*	they, them	*wao*

Demonstratives

Instead of *yeye* and *wao*, Swahilis often use these demonstratives:

| this person | *huyu* | these persons | *hawa* |
| that person | *yule* | those persons | *wale* |

All-purpose demonstratives for things are:

| this (thing) | *hii* | these (things) | *hizi* |
| that (thing) | *ile* | those (things) | *zile* |

To Be

In English, 'to be' is a verb. In Swahili, the various senses of 'to be' take special constructions.

'To be something' is *ni*. The negative, 'not to be something' is *si*.

He is poor.	*yeye ni maskini*
He is John.	*yeye ni John*
John is not rich.	*john si tajiri*
He is not rich.	*yeye si tajiri*

The *ni* can be omitted without change of meaning. The *si* cannot be dropped.

John is poor.   *john maskini*

'To be in or at a place' is subject marker plus *ko*. 'Not to be in or at a place' is negative subject marker plus *ko*. In this case the subject marker for he/she is *yu*. Negative is *hayu*.

		subject marker	ko	
She is in Kenya.		*yu*	*ko kenya*	– *yuko kenya*
Mary is in Kenya.	*mary*	*yu*	*ko kenya*	– *mary yuko kenya*
I am not in Uganda.		*si*	*ko uganda*	– *siko uganda*
She is not in Uganda.		*hayu*	*ko uganda*	– *hayuko uganda*

'To be with' is how one says 'to have' in Swahili. This is subject marker plus *na*, the word used for 'and' or ' with'. 'Not to have', is the negative subject marker plus *na*.

		subject marker	na	
I have a ticket		*ni*	*na tikiti*	– *nina tikiti*
She has a ticket		*a*	*na tikiti*	– *ana tikiti*
Mary has a ticket	*mary*	*a*	*na tikiti*	– *mary ana tikiti*
I don't have a ticket		*si*	*na tikiti*	– *sina tikiti*

Nouns

Swahili divides its nouns into a number of noun-classes, which are distinguished by various prefixes. For survival Swahili purposes there are two important classes, *m-wa* and *n-n*. Whatever the class membership of the noun, if you use *m-wa* prefixes for all persons, and *n-n* prefixes for all things, you will be understood. Don't worry too much about the proper form of the prefix, for it's not the kind of mistake that will confuse your listeners as long as you include the noun that you are talking about.

noun & adjective prefixes		examples		subject prefixes	
singular	plural			singular	plural
m	wa	*mtoto* child	*watoto* children	ni, u, a	tu, m, wa
n	n	*nyumba* house	*nyumba* houses	i	zi

If you are feeling really brave you could try adding another three noun classes to your inventory:

noun & adjective prefixes		examples		subject prefixes	
singular	plural			singular	plural
m	mi	*mti* tree	*miti* trees	u	i
ki	vi	*kitu* thing	*vitu* things	ki	vi
ji	ma	*jicho* eye	*macho* eyes	li	ya

And for the truly unflinching, there are four more which don't differentiate between singular and plural:

noun & adjective prefixes singular & plural	examples	subject prefixes singular & plural
u	*uzuri* goodness	*m*
ku	*kule*	*ku*
pa	*pale*	*pa*
mu	*mle* there (different kinds of space)	*mu*

Possessives

As is the case with nouns, you will be understood if you use the wrong prefixes. Context is what is important. The prefix given is for the singular of the *n-n* class.

my, mine	*yangu*	our, ours	*yetu*
your, yours	*yako*	your, yours (pl)	*yenu*
his, her, hers	*yake*	their, theirs	*yao*

Possessives follow the item possessed.

his wife	*bibi yake*

Adjectives

Adjectives follow the noun, for example:

a big house	*nyumba kubwa*
a ripe banana	*ndizi mbivu*

Some adjectives do not take prefixes and others do, so in this book they are simply presented in the form which is most likely to be useful.

cheap	*rahisi*
expensive	*ghali*
Swahili	*mswahili*
European (including –American & Australian)	*mzungu*
African	*mwafrika*
good, nice,	*mzuri*
bad	*mbaya*
big	*mkubwa*
small	*mdogo*
tall, long	*mrefu*
short	*mfupi*
foreign, strange	*mgeni*
many	*nyingi*
other	*nyingine*
few	*chache*

Prepositions & Conjunctions

and, with	*na*
to, by	*kwa*
of (m-wa)	*wa* (pl: *wa*)
of (n-n)	*ya* (pl: *za*)
but	*lakini*
or	*au*
that	*kwamba*
although	*ingawa*
except	*ila*

therefore	*kwa hivyo*
because	*kwa sababu*
because, that is	*manake*
like, if	*kama*

Questions

There is no special form for questions. You can make any statement into a question by raising the pitch of your voice at the end of the sentence as we do in English.

The bus goes to Nairobi.
   basi inakwenda nairobi
Does this bus go to Nairobi?
   basi inakwenda nairobi?

There are a number of interrogative words as well. In general they go at the end of the sentence.

Interrogative words

who	*nani*
what	*nini*
which, what, what kind	*gani*
why	*kwa nini*
when (what time)	*saa ngapi*
when (what day)	*siku gani*
how	*vipi* (or) *namna gani*
where	*wapi*
how many	*ngapi*

| What kind do you want? | *unataka aina gani?* |
| What is this? | *hii ni nini?* |

And finally a Swahili proverb:

haba na haba hujaza kibaba
  'Little and little fill the *kibaba*-measure'.
  Doing things a bit at a time will get you to where you
  want to be.

Greetings & Civilities

Hello.
habari

I'm fine.
mzuri

Thank you.
asante

Goodbye.
kwa heri

Greetings are more important in Swahili than English, and perhaps for that reason they can be very long and complicated. It is undoubtedly more common to greet strangers than it is in English. Almost all social interactions are prefaced by a greeting. If, say, you would like to ask directions of a man on the street, greet him and then ask the directions. Greeting him is the equivalent of saying, as you would in English, 'excuse me, Sir, can you tell me........'. It is generally considered to be rude not to greet someone who you are going to speak to, no matter what the situation. A nod and a smile are not enough and indeed without the spoken greeting, it may be misconstrued as your laughing at them.

A woman, however, need never initiate or return greetings from a man, unless you know the person well or you want to ask a question. In fact, returning the greeting of a strange man could be construed as a 'come-on'.

Walking hand in hand is a common show of simple friendship among many groups of African men. Men and women never walk hand in hand or otherwise show any physical sign of affection in public. Visitors should keep this in mind and realise that contact or kissing in public may be seen by locals as quite vulgar behaviour.

Forms of Address

Bibi is a term of respect used to address and refer to women. As well as having the meaning 'madam, lady, miss', it can mean 'grandmother' or 'wife' (pl: *mabibi* or *bibi).*

Mama is a term of great respect for women. It literally means 'mother' and is a normal term used to address and refer to older women. It is inappropriate to use to a woman who has no children and thus *bibi*, a more general term, is used throughout this book (pl: *mama).*

Bwana is a term of respect for men. It means 'sir' or 'mister'. It can also mean 'husband' or 'owner'. *Bwana mkubwa* – 'big *bwana*' is used sometimes to refer to the highest ranking man in a group (pl: *mabwana).*

Mzee means 'elder' or 'old person'. It can be a term of great respect, as is often afforded to age, or it may simply be a description of having lived for many years. It can also mean 'parent'. Although a man or a woman may be referred to as an *mzee*, only men are addressed as such, older women normally being addressed *mama* (pl: *wazee).*

Rafiki means 'friend'. 'My friend' is *rafiki yangu* (pl: *marafiki* or *rafiki).*

If you can remember to, always use a title or name and not just a greeting.

Greetings

There are two basic kinds of greetings: those based on *habari*, 'news'; and those based on *jambo*, 'matter'.

Habari greetings are the simpler.
Hello, Sir (literally 'news?, Sir')
  habari, bwana
Hello, Madam
  habari, bibi

the reply is:
Hello, I'm fine (literally 'good').
  mzuri (In Tanzania: *nzuri*)

There are many different things one can ask the news of, but the reply is always *mzuri*. This is the case even when things are not fine. If you feel compelled to say that something is wrong, say *mzuri, lakini........*, that is, 'fine, but........' and say what the matter is.

Hello, Sir, what's (how's) your news?
  habari yako, bwana?
Hello, Sir, what's the news of today?
  habari ya leo, bwana?
Fine.
  mzuri

Or for a bit more embellishment:
Just fine.
  mzuri, tu
Very fine.
  mzuri sana

Jambo greetings change according to number and person.
Jambo means 'matter' or 'problem'.
Hello, Sir. (literally 'you have nothing the matter?')
  hujambo, bwana
I'm fine, Madam. ('I have nothing the matter')
  sijambo, bibi
Hello, Gentlemen.
  hamjambo, mabwana
We're fine, Madam.
  hatujambo, bibi
How are the children? (literally 'they have nothing the matter?)
  hawajambo watoto?
They are fine, Madam.
  hawajambo, bibi

You will also hear a short form used when speaking to tourists who are presumed not to be able to learn anything but the most basic speech.
Hello.
  jambo
Hello. (reply)
  jambo

Groups of children will chant this word when they see a white person, so thoroughly do they associate it with tourists. In Zanzibar one can hear children chant *jambo, mzungu, piga picha* 'jambo, white person, go take a photograph'.

Muslim greetings
Peace be upon you.
  asalaamu alekum

Normally said by the person entering, approaching, or passing. The reply is:
And upon you, peace.
  wa alekum salaam

Another phrase commonly used by Muslims is
If God wills it.
  inshallah

This may be said about virtually any situation the speaker wishes to come to pass, verbally acknowledging that all things are dependent on the will of Allah.
We'll see each other tomorrow.
  tutaonana kesho inshallah

It's probably best to avoid using *inshallah*, as it is easy to misuse; and if you do misuse it, it may unfortunately seem as if you are trying to deliberately insult your listeners.

Of course you will not greet everyone you meet in towns or cities, but in rural areas greetings are the rule.

When approaching a settled area or village greet the people you meet on the path or who you see sitting outside their houses. Remember to use the plural forms of greetings to more than one person.

Children being greeted may get quite excited and even aggressive for they are not customarily included in greetings by adults.

Other Civilities
Goodbye
  kwa heri
To more than one person
  kwa herini

Goodbye and see you again. (farewell)
  kwa heri ya kuonana
We'll see each other again. (see you again)
  tutaonana
See you again tomorrow.
  tutaonana kesho

Very often people preface *kwa heri* by saying *haya*, 'OK, all
right' as if to show that the meeting was successful and is now
completed. People will sometimes use *haya* for 'goodbye'
even without *kwa heri*.

Please (be so kind as to)
  tafadhali
To more than one person
  tafadhalini

Actually *tafadhali* is much more polite than the perfunctory
'please' (or 'would you' or 'could you') that English speakers
put in front of all requests and thus *tafadhali* is best used
when one is actually asking for a favour. It is normally used
with the person's name or title, like *bwana*.

Please (do me a great favour)
  kwa hisani yako
To more than one person
  kwa hisani yenu

This is even more polite than *tafadhali* and is used only when
one is truly coaxing, or asking for a real favour. Normally
used with a name or title.

Thank you.
  asante
Thank you very much.
  asante sana
To more than one person
  asanteni asanteni sana

Asante is most appropriate to show appreciation for a favour or approval of a job well done, as opposed to the perfunctory 'thank you' English speakers use, say, when being served in shops or restaurants.

Forgive me.
  samahani
To more than one person
  samahani

This is not used as an attention-getter, as in English, 'excuse me, mister,' but rather to actually ask forgiveness for a mistake.

Please let me pass.
  tafadhali nipite or *hodi*

In English one says 'excuse me' as one threads through a crowd or tries to move on a packed bus. Normally in Swahili one does not say anything in this situation.

I say!
  ebu or *hallo*

This draws attention, say to flag someone down like a waiter, but to call *weita!* is more common. Upcountry, people call *we* a short form of *wewe* 'you'. To use *we* is considered extremely impolite by coastal people, like English 'hey, you!' Don't use *we*.

Consolations, that's so unfortunate.
  pole
To more than one person
  poleni

This is said when something untoward happens to someone. You may say *pole, bwana* to someone who slips on the street, or who has suffered an accident or death in the family or who is ill. Contrast the English word 'sorry' which if said in many of these situations would suggest that one had caused the situations. *Sori*, is, however, a popular translation of *pole*, so that if you stumble, or almost drop a package on the street, you will hear passers-by telling you *sori, sori*. They are expressing their condolences, not their regret for having caused the situation.

  The response to *pole* is *asante* 'thank you', or, if one is ill, *nitapoa tu*, 'I'll be better'.

Sleep well. (literally 'sleep in peace')
  lala salama
To more than one person
  laleni salama

Hodi
If your intent is to enter a homestead or a house, approach leisurely, and loudly say *hodi* as you approach. If you do not

hear a reply, yell *hodi* again once or twice. If you still hear no reply, it means that no one is in, or that you have come at an inconvenient time.

The reply to your *hodi* is a *hodi* back, or more often *karibu*, which means 'be welcome'. Both mean that you are being welcomed in.

Small Talk

Names

Traditionally, among both Muslim and non-Muslim people, one's 'name' was what we call one's 'first' name or 'Christian' name. The next name was that of one's father, and the next that of his father, so that Ali Omar Ali is Ali, son of Omar, son of Ali. Swahili names also use *bin*, 'son of', thus Ali bin Omar is Ali son of Omar.

What is your name?	*jina lako nani?*
My name is	*jina langu ni ....*
Where are you from?	*unatoka wapi?*
I come from	*mimi ninatoka ....*
America	*amerika*
Australia	*australia*
England	*uingereza*
The UK	*yu kei*
Canada	*kanada*
Germany	*ujerumani*
Switzerland	*uswisi*
France	*ufaransa*
Kenya	*kenya*
Tanzania	*tanzania*
Uganda	*uganda*
Zanzibar	*unguja*
South America	*amerika ya kusini*
Africa	*afrika*
East Africa	*africa ya mashariki*
Europe	*ulaya*

Where in America/England? *wapi amerika/uingereza?*

Unatoka wapi? can also mean 'where are you on your way from, right now?', and is a very polite thing to ask of a person.

Where are you coming from?	*unatoka wapi?*
I'm coming from	*mimi ninatoka ....*
the house	*nyumbani*
the gardens or the rural area	*shambani*
the forest	*mwituni*
town	*mjini*
drawing water	*kuteka maji*
the cinema (the movies)	*sinema*
school	*skuli* or *shuleni*

It is polite to ask the news of the place one has just come from.

How are things in ....?	*habari ya ....?*
town	*mjini*
England	*uingereza*
Fine.	*mzuri*

(Also see *habari* greetings in Greetings chapter.)

What work do you do?	*unafanya kazi gani?*
I am a	*mimi ni ....*
teacher	*mwalimu*
student	*mwanafunzi*
carpenter	*seremala*
farmer	*mkulima*
lawyer	*wakili* or *mwanasheria*
I work in a	*ninafanya kazi kwa ....*
bank	*benki*
factory	*kiwanda*
school	*skuli*
restaurant	*hoteli ya chakula*
hotel	*'lodging'*
	or *hoteli ya kulalia*

Some Useful Phrases

I am happy.
nimefurahi
No problem.
hakuna matata
Let's go.
twende
That's up to you.
shauri yako
Swear to God.
haki ya mungu
It's God's will.
shauri ya mungu
Where do you live?
unakaa wapi?

Now I live in Lamu, but my homeland is Machakos.
sasa ninakaa lamu lakini kwetu ni machakos
Now I live in Kenya, but my homeland is Australia.
sasa ninakaa kenya lakini kwetu ni australia
Are you married? (when asking a man)
umeshaoa bibi?
Are you married? (when asking a woman)
umeshaolewa na bwana?
Yes.
ndiyo
No.
hapana
Do you have children?
una watoto?
How many children do you have?
una watoto wangapi?
Is your wife here?
bibi yako yuko hapa?
My wife is in Europe.
bibi yangu yuko ulaya
Is your husband here?
bwana yako yuko hapa?
Where are your mother and father?
baba na mama wako wapi?
Does he/she live there?
yeye anakaa huko?
I live here because of work.
mimi ninakaa hapa shauri ya kazi
I live here because of school.
mimi ninakaa hapa shauri ya kusoma skuli
I go to school in Machakos.
mimi ninasoma skuli machakos

I have no siblings.
  mimi sina ndugu
I have many siblings.
  mimi nina ndugu wengi
Please share our food. ('be welcome to food')
  karibu chakula
Fine/OK
  haya
No thanks, I'm full.
  asante nimeshiba
Thanks so much for inviting me.
  asante sana kunikaribisha

Note: Thanking people for the meal could be construed as saying it was only the food that was good. Better to thank them for their hospitality.

Shall I take a picture?
  nitapiga picha?
Do you like Kenya?
  unapenda kenya?
I like Kenya very much.
  ninapenda sana kenya
Let's dance.
  twende tukacheze

Getting Around

Public Transport

Taxis They come in all sizes, shapes, and degrees of ancientness or spiffiness. None of them have meters so you must bargain with the driver and be sure to agree on a price before you get in the car.

On other types of public transport there is no bargaining. Everyone pays the same fixed price.

Peugeots These are long-distance shared taxis. They are generally white, nine-seater peugeot station wagons (estate wagons). Keep in mind that when you get in, someone will take your bag and load it in the back or on top of the car. Make sure it's in the same car you're travelling in.

Matatus These are privately owned vans, or small pick-up trucks. They normally follow the same routes as buses, and charge the same or a bit more. They routinely load many more people on board than you would ever think could fit, and the drivers can be rather reckless.

Hitchhiking It is fairly easy to hitchhike on main roads where there are frequent private vehicles. On smaller roads if any vehicles pass you they may already be full to bursting. If not you might offer some money or a gift for the ride.

In East Africa, when night falls, traffic is almost certain to virtually cease and you may be stranded quite literally in the middle of nowhere. A good rule of thumb would be not to hitchhike at night unless it's a real emergency. It is not recommended for a woman to hitchhike alone at any time.

Asking Directions

If you would like to ask directions of someone on the street, start with a greeting and then ask the directions. It would be **extremely** impolite to begin speaking to someone on the street without a greeting first.

Hello, Sir.	*habari, bwana*
Hello, Madam.	*habari, bibi*

The person will reply:

Hello, I'm fine.	*mzuri*

When you are headed somewhere, it is probably a good idea to explain your request for a 'bus station' or whatever with a statement as to where you want to go. There may be several bus stations, or different sections within even a seemingly small station.

I want to go to	*mimi nataka kwenda* ....
I am going to	*mimi nakwenda* ....
How much to go to	*shilingi ngapi kwenda* ....
Where is	*wapi* ....
the bus station	*stesheni ya basi*
Matatu station	*stesheni ya matatu*
the train station	*stesheni ya treni*
the airport	*kiwanja cha ndege*
a taxi	*teksi*
a Mombasa bus	*basi ya mombasa*
a vehicle to Mombasa	*gari ya mombasa*
a car (a shared taxi) to Mombasa	*gari ndogo ya mombasa*
a bus stop	*kituo cha basi*

Some useful phrases

Where are you going?
  unakwenda wapi?
I am going to Lamu.
  mimi nakwenda lamu
Is there a vehicle that goes to Moshi?
  kuna gari ya kwenda moshi?
Not until tomorrow.
  hakuna mpaka kesho
I want a taxi to go to........
  mimi nataka teksi ya kwenda........
I want the Peugeot to........
  nataka peugeot ya........
Is there a boat to........?
  kuna meli ya kwenda ....?
I want to buy a ticket now.
  mimi nataka kukata tikiti sasa
Can I reserve a place?
  naweza kuandikisha nafasi?
How much is a ticket to Mombasa?
  tikiti ya Mombasa ni bei gani?

How long does the trip take?
  safari inachukua muda gani?
When does the bus to Mombasa leave?
  basi ya Mombasa inakwenda saa ngapi?

Remember English time and Swahili time are six hours different. It would be wise to read the Time & Dates chapter before you try to read any bus timetables.

What time do we arrive?
  tutafika saa ngapi?
What day do we arrive?
  tutafika siku gani?
When is the last bus?
  saa ngapi basi ya mwisho?
Can we get food on the road?
  tunaweza kupata chakula njiani?
I don't know.
  sijui
I'm sorry, I don't understand.
  nisamehe sifahamu
Now I understand.
  sasa nafahamu
Where is a porter?
  wapi hamali?
Who is the conductor?
  nani kandakta?
Where is the driver?
  wapi dereva?
Is someone sitting here?
  kuna mtu hapa?
There is someone here.
  kuna mtu hapa
Is there space here?
  iko nafasi hapa?
Is this the bus to Mombasa?
  hii basi ya mombasa?
How long do we stop here?
  tunasimama hapa muda gani?
Will this bus pass Katheka Kai?
  hii basi itapita katheka kai?

Where do I get off?
  nishuke wapi?
Please tell me when we get there.
  tafadhali niambie tukifika
Not yet.
  bado
Get off here.
  shuka hapa
Is this the way to........?
  hii njia ya........?
Where does this road go to?
  njia hii ni ya kwenda wapi?
The road is out.
  njia imeharibika
I am lost.
  nimepotea
I live at the New Kenya Hotel.
  ninakaa new kenya hotel
Over there.
  pale
In the middle.
  katikati
Drive slowly.
  endesha pole pole
Drive quickly.
  endesha upesi
Wait a bit.
  ngoja kidogo
Let's go.
  twende
I want to go to the police.
  nataka kwenda kwa polisi

Some useful words
one-way
  kwenda tu
round trip (return)
  kwenda na kurudi
now
  sasa
left
  kwa kushoto
right
  kwa kulia
straight
  moja kwa moja
stop
  simama
difficult
  vigumu
slowly
  pole pole
quickly
  haraka
totally/entirely
  kabisa
up/above
  juu
down/below
  chini
near
  karibu
far
  mbali

together
  pamoja
in front of
  mbele
behind
  nyumba
in/inside
  ndani
out/outside
  nje
to one side
  kando
in the middle
  katikati
in
  katika
straight
  moja kwa moja
right
  kwa kulia
left
  kwa kushoto

Emergencies
I've been robbed.
  nimeibiwa
I'm sick.
  mimi mgonjwa
I need a doctor.
  nataka daktari
I can't see.
  siwezi kuona

I have missed the........	*nimekosa........*
My bag is on the........	*mzigo wangu uko kwa........*
bus	*basi*
train	*treni*
boat or ferry	*boti*

Some useful phrases

Watch out!
angalia

Leave me alone!
niache

I don't want any.
sitaki

No thanks.
asante

Go away!
nenda zako

Get out!
toka

I'm lost.
nimepotea

Some useful words

danger
hatari

fire
moto

accident
ajali

police
polisi

police officer/guard
  askari
come
  njoo
thief
  mwizi

If you call out *mwizi*, passers-by may try to help. It is worth thinking about the consequences first though, as if a thief is caught, he may be beaten to death. There are often newspaper reports of members of the public resorting to 'mob justice' with the accused being rescued by the police.

Some Swahili Proverbs
haraka haraka haina baraka
  '(In) hurry, hurry, there is no blessing.'

pole pole ndiyo mwendo
  'Slowly slowly is indeed the (proper) path.'

kawia ufike
  'Be late (but) get there.'

shauku nyingi huondoa maarifa
  'Intense desire removes intelligence.'

Accomodation

If you ask for a 'good' hotel in East Africa, you will probably wind up being shown the Hilton or the local equivalent, which is fine if that's what you want. If you want a more reasonably priced place, you will have to be more specific.

All but the most deluxe hotels will show you a room before you commit yourself to taking it. Take advantage of this, and you can avoid unpleasant surprises due to miscommunication.

Be aware that the Swahili word *hoteli* usually means a restaurant, although it can also mean a hotel. Many Swahilis use the word 'lodging' to mean a hotel. It is possible that some people will not know 'lodging', so both *hoteli* and 'lodging' are given.

Before asking anyone where you might find a hotel be sure to greet them. Remember that it is considered impolite to begin speaking to someone without a verbal greeting.

I want a very good hotel.
mimi nataka hoteli (or 'lodging') *nzuri sana*
Is there a hotel close by?
kuna hoteli (or 'lodging') *karibu hapa?*
A not too expensive one.
tena rahisi kidogo

I would like a hotel close to the........	*mimi nataka hoteli karibu na........*
beach	*pwani*
market	*sokoni*
bus station	*stesheni ya basi*
train station	*stesheni ya treni*
game park	*mahali kwa kutazama wanyama*

Note that a 'room' in a house is *chumba*, and although standard Swahili prescribes *chumba* to be used for 'hotel room', the most common word is *rumu*.

Do you have a room for........	*kuna rumu ya........*
one person	*mtu moja*
two people	*watu wawili*
three people	*watu watatu*
four people	*watu wanne*

No, there is none.
hapana or *hakuna*
It is full.
imejaa
Yes.
ndiyo

There is.
  iko
How much is the room?
  rumu ni shilingi ngapi?
I want a bed.
  nataka kitanda
How much is a bed?
  kitanda ni shilingi ngapi?
For one day.
  kwa siku moja
For a week.
  kwa wiki mzima
For a month.
  kwa mwezi

In the room is there a........? *kwenye rumu kuna........?*

shower	*shawa*
water tap	*maji ya mfereji*
toilet	*choo*
bath	*bafu*
fan	*feni* or *banka*

Is there hot water?
  kuna maji ya moto?
At what times?
  saa ngapi?
I'd like to see the room.
  nataka kuona rumu tafadhali
All right/OK (I'll take it).
  haya sawa sawa

I don't want it.
sitaki hii
Is there another?
kuna ingine?
Yes. Let's go.
ndiyo twende
No. Only this.
hapana iko hiyo tu
Thanks anyway.
asantẹ

Where is........?   *wapi........*
  a hotel less expensive than this one
    hotel rahisi kuliko hii
  a hotel more expensive than this one
    hotel ghali kuliko hii

I would like to move into a different room.
  mimi nataka kuhamia rumu ingine
Why?
  kwa nini?
Too much noise.
  kelele nyingi
There's no fan.
  hakuna feni
Odour from the kitchen.
  harufu ya jikoni
Odour from the toilet.
  harufu ya choo
It's very warm.
  kuna joto sana

It's very cold.
  kuna baridi sana
The bed is terrible.
  kitanda kibaya

I'd like to reserve a room.
  nataka kuandikisha rumu
What date?
  tarehe gani?
My wife and I
  mimi na mke wangu
My friend and I
  mimi na rafiki yangu
My family and I
  mimi na jamaa yangu
What number is my room?
  rumu yangu nambari ngapi?
Give me the key, please.
  lete ufunguo
I would like my bill.
  nataka hesabu yangu
I would like to pay now.
  nataka kulipa sasa
I cannot close (or lock) the door.
  siwezi kufunga mlango
I cannot open (or unlock) the door.
  siwezi kufungua mlango

The........ is not clean; please bring me another.
  hii........ si safi; lete ingine
The........ doesn't work. (is broken)
  .... imeharibika

There is no more........
...... *imekwisha*
I need a........
  mimi nataka........
Where is........?
  wapi........?

Some useful words

basin (sink)	*beisini*
bedsheet	*shiti* or *shuka*
blanket	*blanketi*
firewood	*kuni*
glass	*glasi*
hot water	*maji ya moto*
light	*taa*
light bulb	*globu ya taa*
mattress	*godoro*
mosquito coils	*dawa ya mbu ya kuwashia*
mosquito net	*chandalua ya mbu*
pillow	*mto*
pillowcase	*foronya* or *mfuko wa mto*
shower	*shawa*
soap	*sabuni*
tap (faucet)	*mfereji*
toilet	*choo*
toilet paper	*karatasi ya choo*
towel	*tauli*

Put it here.
  weka hapa

On Safari

'Safari' simply means 'journey'. When English borrowed the term from Swahili, it specialised its meaning into 'an expedition, the goal of which is often wild game'.

We would like very much to see ....
    tunataka sana kuona ....
Yesterday we saw ....
    jana tuliona ....
Today we saw ....
    leo tuliona ....

Some useful words

animal	*mnyama*
antelope	*pofu* or *kulungu*
army ants	*siafu*
baboon	*nyani*
bird	*ndege*
bushbaby	*komba*
camel	*ngamia*
centipede	*tandu*
crocodile	*mamba*
dik-dik	*dikidiki*
duiker	*funo* or *mindi*
eland	*pofu*
elephant	*ndovu* or *tembo*
flamingo	*heroe*
fox	*mbweha*
gazelle	*swala* or *swara* or *paa*

giraffe	*twiga*
hartebeest	*kongoni*
hippopotamus	*kiboko*
hyena	*fisi*
insect	*mdudu*
leopard	*chui*
lion	*simba*
monkey	*tumbili*
mosquitoes	*mbu*
ostrich	*mbuni*
python	*chatu*
rhinoceros	*kifaru*
sable antelope	*palahala*
snake	*nyoka*
spider	*buibui*
spitting cobra	*swila*
warthog	*ngiri*
water buffalo	*nyati*
wildebeest or gnu	*nyumbu* or *mbogo*
zebra	*punda milia*

Danger.
   hatari
This one is dangerous.
   huyu hatari
Don't get out of the car!
   usitoke kwa gari! or *garini!* or, upcountry: *hapana toka gari!*
She has babies/pups/cubs.
   ana watoto
Don't annoy the animal!
   usimbue! or, upcountry: *hapana sumbua mnyama!*

Look there.
  tazama pale
What is there?
  iko nini pale?
What animal is that?
  huyo mnyama gani?
A lion and her cubs.
  simba na watoto wake

Weather

Is there rain today?
  kuna mvua leo?
There is rain.
  kuna mvua
It is sunny.
  kuna jua
The sun is fierce.
  jua kali
It is hot.
  kuna joto
It is cold.
  kuna baridi
It is windy.
  kuna upepo

Food

food	*chakula*
water	*maji*

I would like........	*nataka........*
one can of........	*mkebe moja wa........*
one packet of........	*pakiti moja ya........*
one box of........	*boksi moja ya........*
one kg of........	*kilo moja ya........*

Also see the Numbers and Shopping chapters.

Provisions from a General Store *duka*

rice	*mchele*
maize (corn) meal	*unga wa mahindi*
spaghetti	*spageti* or *makaronya* or *tambi*
salt	*chumvi*
sugar	*sukari*
curry powder	*bizari*
coffee	*kahawa*
instant coffee	*nescafe* (brand name)
tea	*chai* or *majani ya chai*
powdered milk	*maziwa ya unga*
margarine	*blue band* (brand name)
cooking fat	*kimbo* (brand name)
flavoured cooking fat	*cowboy* (brand name)
liquid oil	*saladi oil* or *mafuta ya kupikia*

53

tinned (canned) meat	*nyama ya mkebe*
tinned (canned) sardines	*samaki ya mkebe*
egg	*yai* (pl: *mayai*)
vinegar	*siki*
tomato sauce	*tomato* or *tomato sos*
tomato paste	*tomato ya mkebe*
detergent powder	*omo* (brand name)
matches	*kibiriti*
knife	*kisu*
paraffin (kerosene)	*mafuta ya taa*
kidney beans	*maharagwe*
green gram (mung beans)	*pojo*
lentils, chickpeas	*dengu*
cowpea	*kunde*
pigeon pea	*mbaazi*

Spices

black pepper	*pilipili manga*
ginger	*tangawizi*
cardamom	*iliki*
cloves	*karafuu*
cinnamon	*mdalasini*
turmeric	*manjano*
cumin	*bizari nyembamba*
coriander	*dania*

Some useful words

raw	*mbichi*
ripe	*mbivu*
sweet	*tamu*

At the Market   *sokoni*

Fruit and vegetables are usually sold by the pile, *kifungo*.
That is, the seller will put two or more of an item together,
perhaps fewer large ones or more overripe ones for the same
price. Fruit and vegetables may also be sold by the item, or
by weight.

vegetables	*mboga*
fruit	*matunda*
potatoes	*viazi*
onions	*vitunguu*
garlic	*vitunguu saumu*
spinach	*mchicha*
kale	*sukuma wiki*
cabbage	*kabichi*
carrots	*karoti*
tomatoes	*nyanya*
tamarind	*ukwaju*
hot peppers	*pilipili hoho*
green sweet peppers	*pilipili baridi*
lettuce	*salad*
eggplant/aubergine	*biringani*
manioc	*muhogo*
unripe coconut (for drinking)	*dafu*
ripe coconut	*nazi*
limes	*ndimu*
papayas	*paipai*
mangoes	*maembe*
bananas	*ndizi*
oranges	*machungwa*
pineapples	*mananasi*
grapefruits	*madanzi* or *mabalungi*

passion fruit	*pasheni*
watermelon	*tikiti* or *tango*
dates	*tende*
sugar cane	*miwa*
soursop	*stafeli*

How much are these?
  hizi bei gani?
How much is this?
  hii bei gani?

At the Butcher

In many local butcher shops, the two main categories are:

meat with bone	*nyama yenye mafupa*
meat without bone	*nyama bila ya mafupa* or *mnofu*

A cut may also be specified:

a loin cut, often fillet (filet mignon) or sirloin	*sarara*
rib	*nyama ya mbavu*
leg	*nyama ya mguu*
rump	*nyama ya tako*
heart	*moyo*
tongue	*ulimi*
liver	*maini*
chicken	*kuku*
fish	*samaki*
beef	*nyama ya ng'ombe*
pork	*nyama ya nguruwe*
veal	*nyama ya mdama*
goat	*nyama ya mbuzi*
sheep or lamb	*nyama ya kondoo*

Be aware that 'mutton' normally refers to goat's meat.

Is this beef?
  hii nyama ya ng'ombe?
This is goat.
  hii ni nyama ya mbuzi
I would like beef.
  nataka nyama ya ng'ombe.
Give me two kg of fillet steak, please.
  lete kilo mbili ya sarara
How much is a kg of goat meat?
  kilo ya nyama ya mbuzi shilingi ngapi?

At the Fish Market

fish	*samaki*
dried fish	*ng'onda*
shrimp	*kamba* or *kamba mdogo*
lobster	*kamba* or *kamba mkubwa*
crab	*kaa*
octopus	*pweza*
cuttlefish, squid	*ngisi*

There are of course many varieties of finfish; these kinds are especially good eating:

kingfish	*nguru*
shark	*papa*
grouper	*tewa*
emperor's glory snapper	*changu*
mullet	*mkesi*
rabbit fish	*tasi* or *tafi*
amberjack, pompano	*kole kole*

At a Restaurant

Please note that menu terms can mean different things from one region to another, or even from one restaurant to another on the same street. So if you order something and it turns out different from what you expected, remember it can also happen in New York and Melbourne too.

Where is a restaurant?
   wapi hoteli ya chakula?
I would like........
   nataka........
and also........
   na........ pia
And something else?
   na kitu kingine?
What will you drink?
   utakunywa nini?

the menu	*menyu*
coffee	*kahawa*
black coffee	*kahawa bila maziwa* or *kahawa kavu*
instant coffee in hot milk	*kahawa maziwa* or *kofi*

Tea served in African-style restaurants is usually brewed tea served already mixed with milk and sugar.

tea	*chai*
tea with relatively more milk	*chai spesheli*
black tea, ie, without milk	*chai kavu*
soda	*soda*
cold soda	*soda baridi*

What kind of cold soda is there?
kuna soda gani baridi?

The word for water is *maji*, which actually means liquid.

water (drinking)	*maji ya kunywa*
cold water	*maji baridi*
hot water	*maji ya moto*
fruit juice	*maji ya tamu*
orange juice	*maji ya machungwa*
lime juice	*maji ya ndimu*
pineapple juice	*maji ya nanasi*

What kind of fruit juice is there?
kuna maji ya tamu aina gani?
I don't want tinned (canned).
sitaki ya mkebe

The national snack of Kenya, and most of East Africa, is
samosa, a deep-fried triangular pie filled with meat mixed
with vegetables or, in some places, vegetables alone. On the
coast it is served with lime. People often bite off a corner of
the samosa and squeeze lime juice inside onto the filling.

samosa	*samosa* or *sambusa*
vegetable samosa	*samosa ya mboga*
meat samosa	*samosa ya nyama*
lime	*ndimu*

Both these dishes are rice, with some meat for flavouring:

layered rice and meat dish	*biriani*
rice and meat cooked together	*pilau* or *plau*

biriani with goat meat	*biriani ya mbuzi*
biriani with chicken	*biriani ya kuku*
biriani with fish	*biriani ya samaki*
pilau with goat meat	*pilau ya mbuzi*
curry	*mchuzi* or *kari*

Mchuzi is also a general word for 'sauce' or 'gravy' and by extension, although rarely, 'soup'.

chicken curry	*mchuzi wa kuku*
beef curry	*mchuzi wa ng'ombe*
mincemeat (ground meat) curry	*kima*
meatball curry	*kofta kari*
masala (which in East Africa differs from curry most obviously in being heavier and drier)	*masala* or *mchuzi mzito*

Note that *masala* is not a dish cooked in marsala wine, but refers to a combination of spices.

Indian flat bread	*chapati*
beef stew	*karanga*
beef stew with less beef	*ng'ombe*

Soup is a popular breakfast on the coast and restaurants will have 'special morning soup' as a menu term. It's usually made from goat meat.

soup	*supu*
chicken soup	*supu ya kuku*

roast meat on a skewer	*mishkaki* or *mishakiki*
roast ground meat on a skewer	*kababu* or *kofta kabab*

Mkate Wa Mayai

Literally 'bread of eggs', there are two distinct items sold under the name *mkate wa mayai*. The less common is 'French toast', bread dipped in an egg and milk mixture and then fried.

The more common is a dish usually served only in the evening, made on a large *chuma chapati*, an iron chapati griddle, heated over a charcoal fire. A square of rolled-out dough is fried until it forms a crisp base crust, and a mixture of cooked ground meat, onions and spices is heaped onto this base. Then one or more eggs are broken over and mixed into the meat mixture. The whole is topped with a larger piece of dough and flipped over, the edges of the larger piece folded over to seal the meat and egg mixture inside. The *mkate wa mayai* is then slowly fried to a golden brown while the egg sets and the flavours blend inside.

You'll know a good place because instead of having a pile of *mkate wa mayai* lying around precooked, they will cook the dish to order, and there will be a group of customers crowded around in front of the restaurant watching the cook assemble and cook theirs.

Beer

Beer is served chilled (cold), or at room-temperature (warm). One normally orders by brand and temperature.

I'd like a cold Tusker.
nataka tuska baridi
I'd like two cold Pilsners and a warm Tusker Export.
nataka pilsner mbili baridi na tuska export moto

beer	*bia* or *pombe*
cold	*baridi*
warm	*moto*
any alchoholic beverage, but especially local brew	*pombe* or *tembo*
bottle	*chupa*
opener	*kifunguo*
one	*moja*
two	*mbili*
three	*tatu*

Some Useful Phrases

I would like prawn curry.
mimi nataka mchuzi wa kamba
We have run out of prawns.
kamba zimekwisha (literally 'prawns they are finished')
What is there to eat?
kuna chakula gani?
There is fish curry with chapati.
iko mchuzi wa samaki na chapati
This has cooled.
hii imepoa

Please heat it up.
tafadhali pasha moto

I cannot eat meat.
siwezi kula nyama

I cannot eat meat or fish.
siwezi kula nyama wala samaki

I cannot eat meat, fish, or eggs.
siwezi kula nyama samaki wala mayai

I can only eat vegetables.
naweza kula mboga peke yake

I can eat fish.
naweza kula samaki

I can eat eggs.
naweza kula mayai

How much do I owe?
deni yangu ngapi?

Some Useful Words

teaspoon	*kijiko*
soupspoon	*kijiko cha supu*
fork	*uma*
knife	*kisu*
cloth napkin	*kitambaa*
paper napkin	*karatasi ya mkono*
plate	*sahani*
glass	*glasi* or *bilauri*
cup	*kikombe*
platter, tray	*sinia*

If you want your food to take away (take out), or want to take what you haven't finished with you, you can ask for the food to be wrapped up.

Wrap it in paper.
funga kwa karatasi
Wrap it for me.
nifungie

Shopping

Money

The currencies of Kenya, Tanzania and Uganda are all called shillings. Don't let this fool you in to believing that they are the same, because there is tremendous variation in exchange rate and buying power from country to country.

shilling		*shilingi*
1 shilling	(written 1/=)	*shilingi moja*
2 shillings	(2/=)	*shilingi mbili*
200 shillings	(200/=)	*shilingi mia mbili*

Shillings are divided into 100 cents.

10 cents	(-/10)	*senti kumi*
45 cents	(-/45)	*senti arobaini na tano*

In Kenya shillings are divided into 5-cent, 10-cent, and 50-cent units.

5 cents	(-/05)	*ndururu*
10 cents	(-/10)	*peni moja* ('one penny')
50 cents	(-/50)	*sumuni* (=*peni tano* 'five pennies')
15 cents	(-/15)	*peni moja na ndururu*
30 cents	(-/30)	*peni tatu*
45 cents	(-/45)	*peni nne na ndururu*
55 cents	(-/55)	*peni tano na ndururu*

one shilling 55 cents (1/55)	*shilingi moja peni tano na*
	ndururu

Shops & Markets
Directions to shops & markets

Always greet a person before asking a question. It would be impolite to begin speaking to someone on the street without a greeting first. Also, on walking into a shop it is polite to greet the shop keeper before you begin to make your purchase (not all shoppers do this).

Hello, Sir	*habari bwana*
Hello, Madam	*habari bibi*

The person will reply:

Hello, I'm fine	*mzuri*

Then, to ask where something is, you can say:

I am looking for........	*mimi natafuta........*

A simpler way to get the same information is:

Where is the........?	*wapi........?*
bakery	*duka la mkate*
book store	*duka la vitabu*
camera store or photographer	*duka la kupiga picha*
carpenter	*seremala* or *fundi wa mbao*
clothing store	*duka la nguo*
craftsman	*fundi*
food store	*duka la chakula*
general store	*duka*
hardware store	*duka la vyombo vya chuma*

marketplace	*sokoni*
music store	*duka la muziki*
pharmacy	*duka la madawa*
shoe repairer	*fundi wa viatu*
shoe store	*duka la viatu*
spice shop	*duka la madawa*
tailor	*mshonaji*
town	*mjini* or *tauni*
watch repairer	*fundi wa saa*

I want to buy........
mimi nataka kununua........
I want to get........
mimi nataka kupata........
I want (ie, I would like)........
mimi nataka........

Some useful words

pants	*suruali*
shirt	*shati*
shoes	*viatu*
underpants	*suruali ya ndani*
socks	*soksi*
brassiere	*sidiria*
coat	*koti*
shorts	*suruali fupi*
sweater	*sueta* (upcountry: *fulana*)
t-shirt	*fulana* (upcountry: *shati ya ndani*)
rubber sandals (flip-flops)	*viatu vya mpira* or *champale*
woodcarvings	*sanamu*
a present	*zawadi*

knife	*kisu*
machete, bush knife	*panga*
pail, bucket	*ndoo*
large basin	*karai*
of metal	*ya chuma*
of plastic	*ya plastiki* or *ya nailon*
of wood	*ya mbao*
soap	*sabuni*
toothpaste	*dawa ya meno*
toothbrush	*mswaki*
mirror	*kioo*
razor	*kijembe*
comb	*kitana*
toilet paper	*karatasi ya choo*
clothes detergent	*omo* (a brand name)
thread	*uzi*
needle	*sindano*
insect spray	*dawa ya mdudu*
mosquito coils	*dawa ya mbu ya kuwashia*
matches	*kibiriti*
candles	*mishumaa*
spirit (rubbing alcohol, fuel alcohol)	*spiriti*
paraffin (kerosene)	*mafuta ya taa*
petrol	*petroli*
cooking oil	*saladi oil* or *mafuta ya kupikia*
rectangle of cloth with bordered pattern with a saying on it, worn by women as a shawl or apron, by men to sleep in	*kanga*

sarong, loincloth sewed   *saruni*
  into a tube, worn by men
  only

Some Useful Phrases

Do you have........? /Is there........?
  kuna........?
There is.
  iko
No, it's finished/out of stock.
  kwisha
There is none.
  hakuna (In Tanzania: *hamna*)
How much is this?
  hii bei gani?
How much is that?
  ile bei gani
Which one?
  ipi?
This one.
  hii
That one.
  ile
To the left.
  kwa kushoto
To the right.
  kwa kulia
I want one the same as this.
  nataka sawa sawa na hii
I want one like this.
  nataka kama hii

I want that one.
  nataka ile
I want this one.
  nataka hii
I don't want this one.
  sitaki hii
Show me another.
  nionyeshe ingine
This is too big.
  hii kubwa
This is too small.
  hii ndogo
What does this do?
  hii kazi yake nini?
Show me.
  nionyeshe
I want a different kind/brand.
  nataka aina ingine
I want a less expensive one.
  nataka ingine raisi zaidi

Yes	*ndiyo*
No	*hapana*
All right/OK	*haya*
All right/OK	*sawa sawa* (also means 'the same')

Bargaining
Fixed price (ie, no bargaining)
  bei moja
How much?
  bei gani?

Your price is too high.
bei yako ghali
This is a very high price.
hii ni bei ghali sana
Charge me the usual price.
nipe bei ya kawaida
What is your last price?
bei ya mwisho ngapi?
If I buy two?
nikichukua mbili?
Reduce the price, Sir.
punguza bei bwana

Take off a little (from the price), Sir.
toa kidogo bwana
Increase (what you are giving me) a little.
ongeza kidogo bwana

Some Useful Words
small amount
kidogo
many
nyingi
just, only
tu
also
pia
very much, very
sana
more
zaidi
maybe
labda

Health

Aside from the general rules of keeping healthy in the tropics (keeping skin very clean, taking all measures to avoid being bitten by mosquitoes, taking anti-malaria medicine, washing hands before eating, not walking barefoot on soil, taking the most immediate care of cuts, having all shots up to date, etc), you must know about the disease **bilharzia** (also called Schistosomiasis). Bilharzia breeds in fresh water, so it is advisable not to come into contact with fresh bodies of water like lakes, rivers, or reservoirs. Bilharzia parasites burrow through human skin that is in contact with infested water. Bilharzia is endemic in East Africa. It is impossible to tell if water is infested by looking at it. Chlorinated water and salt water are safe. Do not swim in fresh water.

I am ill.
  mimi mgonjwa
I want a doctor.
  nataka daktari
I can go to the doctor.
  naweza kwenda kwa daktari
I can't go.
  siwezi kwenda
He/She can't go.
  hawezi kwenda
Could you please call a doctor.
  tafadhali wewe umwite dakari
Please do this favour.
  kwa hisani yako

All right/OK.
  haya
The doctor wasn't there.
  daktari hayuko
The doctor is coming.
  daktari anakuja
Is there a hospital?
  kuna hospitali?
There is not.
  hakuna
There is.
  iko
Show me where the hospital is.
  nionyeshe hospitali iko wapi
I want a taxi.
  nataka taxi
I want a vehicle.
  nataka gari

Bring drinking water.
  lete maji ya kunywa
Bring an empty bucket.
  lete ndoo tupu
Bring some toilet paper.
  lete karatasi ya choo
Bring water to use in the toilet.
  lete maji ya kutumia kwa choo
Please clean here.
  tafadhali safisha hapa
Please clean the toilet.
  tafadhali safisha choo
Thank you very much, Sir.
  asante sana bwana
Thank you very much, Madam.
  asante sana bibi

blood	*damu*
water	*maji*
urine	*mkojo*
faeces	*mavi* or *choo*

Some Useful Phrases

Doctors and chemists (pharmacists) will speak English. You may however need to explain to an intermediary.

For the following phrases, to say 'he' or 'she' instead of 'I', change the first *ni* to *a* – so *nina* becomes *ana*, etc)

Tell him/her........	*mambie........*
I have a fever	*nina homa*
I have diarrhoea	*ninahara*
I have dysentry (blood in stool)	*ninahara damu*
I am vomiting	*ninatapika*
I am coughing	*ninakohoa*
I hurt here	*ninaumwa hapa*
I hurt here inside	*ninaumwa hapa ndani*
I am swelling here	*ninafura hapa*
I am in pain	*ninasikia maumivu*
I feel very hot	*ninasikia moto sana*
I feel very cold	*ninasikia baridi sana*
I have chills	*ninatetemeka*
I was bitten by a snake	*niliumwa na nyoka*
I am pregnant	*nina mimba*
Please hurry	*fanya haraka tafadhali*
I'm sorry/It's really unfortunate	*pole*
Thank you	*asante*
Just rotten luck	*bahati mbaya tu*

Time

day	*siku*
daytime	*mchana*
night–time	*usiku*
morning	*asubuhi*
evening	*jioni*
week	*wiki*
month	*mwezi*
year	*mwaka*

Days

Monday	*jumatatu*
Tuesday	*jumanne*
Wednesday	*jumatano*
Thursday	*alhamisi*
Friday	*ijumaa*
Saturday	*jumamosi*
Sunday	*jumapili*

Ijumaa (Friday) is the Muslim holy day, the day of assembly and the end of the Muslim week.

Months

January	*januari*
February	*februari*
March	*machi*
April	*aprili*
May	*mei*
June	*juni*

July	*julai*
August	*agosti*
September	*septemba*
October	*octoba*
November	*novemba*
December	*desemba*

Present, Past & Future

day after tomorrow	*kesho kutwa*
tomorrow	*kesho*
today	*leo*
yesterday	*jana*
day before yesterday, a few days ago	*juzi*
tomorrow evening	*kesho usiku*
tomorrow morning	*kesho asubuhi*
tonight	*leo usiku*
this morning	*leo asubuhi*
yesterday morning	*jana asubuhi*
yesterday evening	*jana usiku*
next week	*wiki ijayo*
this week	*wiki hii*
last week	*wiki jana*
next month	*mwezi ujao*
this month	*mwezi huu*
last month	*mwezi uliopita*
next year	*mwaka ujao*
this year	*mwaka huu*
last year	*mwaka jana*
later	*baadaye*
not yet	*bado*
in just a minute	*sasa hivi*

now	*sasa*
just before	*hivi sasa*
quite a while ago	*kitambo*
long ago	*zamani*
every day	*kila siku*
always	*siku zote*

Time

Time is told with the word *saa*, which means 'time', 'hour', and 'watch'. *Saa mbili* means 'the second hour'.

Swahili time and western time are six hours apart. The Swahili clock begins counting hours from the beginning of the night (sundown) and the beginning of the day (daybreak). *Saa moja (saa 1) ya asubuhi* is the first hour after the beginning of the day (or 7 am by western reckoning), *saa moja (saa 1) ya jioni* is the first hour after the beginning of the night (or 7 pm).

English hour		Swahili *saa*	
12	midnight	6	*saa sita ya usiku*
1		7	*saa saba ya usiku*
2		8	*saa nane ya usiku*
3		9	*saa tisa ya usiku*
4		10	*saa kumi ya usiku*
5		11	*saa kumi na moja ya usiku*
6	daybreak	12	*saa kumi na mbili ya alfajiri*
7		1	*saa moja ya asubuhi*
8		2	*saa mbili ya asubuhi*
9		3	*saa tatu ya asubuhi*
10		4	*saa nne ya asubuhi*
11		5	*saa tano ya asubuhi*
12	midday	6	*saa sita ya mchana*
1		7	*saa saba ya mchana*
2		8	*saa nane ya alasiri*
3		9	*saa tisa ya alasiri*
4		10	*saa kumi ya alasiri*
5		11	*saa kumi na moja ya jioni*
6	sundown	12	*saa kumi na mbili ya jioni*
7		1	*saa moja ya jioni*
8		2	*saa mbili ya usiku*
9		3	*saa tatu ya usiku*
10		4	*saa nne ya usiku*
11		5	*saa tano ya usiku*
12	midnight	6	*saa sita ya usiku*

What time is it?
  saa ngapi?
Eight o'clock.
  saa mbili (2)
Three o'clock.
  saa tisa

What day of the week is today?
  leo siku gani?
Today is Sunday.
  leo jumapili
What date is today?
  leo tarehe gani?
Today is 3 July.
  leo tarehe tatu mwezi wa julai
I leave on 24 October.
  mimi nitatoka tarehe ishirini na nne mwezi wa oktoba
I will return after two years.
  nitarudi baada ya miaka miwili

Numbers

Cardinal Numbers

0	*sifuri*
1	*moja*
2	*mbili*
3	*tatu*
4	*nne*
5	*tano*
6	*sita*
7	*saba*
8	*nane*
9	*tisa*
10	*kumi*
11	*kumi na moja*
12	*kumi na mbili*
13	*kumi na tatu*
14	*kumi na nne*
15	*kumi na tano*
16	*kumi na sita*
17	*kumi na saba*
18	*kumi na nane*
19	*kumi na tisa*
20	*ishirini*
21	*ishirini na moja*
22	*ishirini na mbili*
30	*thelathini*
31	*thelathini na moja*
40	*arobaini*
50	*hamsini*

60	*sitini*
70	*sabini*
80	*themanini*
90	*tisini*
100	*mia*
101	*mia na moja*
106	*mia na sita*
154	*mia na hamsini na tano*
200	*mia mbili*
300	*mia tatu*
1000	*elfu*
2000	*elfu mbili*
100, 000	*laki*
1,000,000	*milioni*

one quarter – ¼	*robo*
one half – ½	*nusu*

Ordinals

first	*ya kwanza*
second	*ya pili*
third	*ya tatu*
fourth	*ya nne*
fifth	*ya tano*
sixth	*ya sita*
seventh	*ya saba*
eighth	*ya nane*
ninth	*ya tisa*
tenth	*ya kumi*

Some of the cardinals, and the *ya* of the ordinals, change depending on the noun class of the thing being counted or ordered. The forms given are for *n-n* class, yet will be understood perfectly well if you (ungrammatically) use them to count items in other noun classes. Indeed, upcountry no other agreements are used.

Both cardinals and ordinals follow the item(s) being counted.

Vocabulary

A

able, be (v) – *weza*
above – *juu ya*
absolutely – *kabisa*
address – *anwani*
again – *tena*
ago – *iliyopita*
agree (v) – *kubali*
airport – *kiwanja cha ndege*
alcohol – *spiriti*
all – *yote*
almost – *karibu*
alone – *peke yake*
also – *pia*
always – *saa zote*
and – *na*
animal – *mnyama*
annoy – *sumbua*
another – *ingine*
answer (v & n) – *jibu*
any – *yo yote*
anything – *kitu cho chote*
apart – *mbali*
arm – *mkono*
arrive – *fika*
as – *kama*
ask (v) – *uliza*
at – *kwa*

B

bag – *mfuko*
bank – *benki*
bathe (v) – *kuoga*
bathroom, toilet – *choo*
be happy (v) – *furahi*
be sad (v) – *sikitika*
beach – *pwani, ufuoni*
because – *kwa sababu*
bed – *kitanda*
beef – *nyama ya ng'ombe*
beer – *pombe, bia*
before – *kabla ya*
begin (v) – *anza*
below – *chini*
best – *nzuri kabisa*
better – *nzuri zaidi*
beverage – *kinywaji*
big – *kubwa*
bird – *ndege*
bite (v) – *uma*
bitten, be (v) – *umwa*
black – *mweusi*
blanket – *blanketi*
blood – *damu*
blue – *buluu*
board – *mbao*
boat – *boti*
bone – *mfupa*
book – *kitabu*
both – *yote mbili*
bottle – *chupa*

box – *boksi/kartoni*
brand – *aina*
bread – *mkate*
bring (v) – *leta*
broken, be (v) – *vunjika*
brown – *mwekundu, rangi ya kahawa*
bucket – *ndoo*
bulb – *globu*
bus – *basi*
bush country – *porini*
but – *lakini*
buy (v) – *nunua*
by – *kwa*

C

call (v) – *ita*
camera – *kamera*
can, tin – *mkebe*
can, be able (v) – *weza*
candles – *mishumaa*
canned – *ya mkebe*
car – *gari*
certainly – *kwa hakika*
charcoal – *makaa*
chicken – *kuku*
child – *mtoto*
children – *watoto*
chilled – *ya baridi*
Christian – *mkristo*
cigarettes – *sigara*
cinema, movies – *sinema*
clean – *safi*

close – *karibu*
cloth – *kitambaa*
clothes – *nguo*
coast – *pwani*
coat – *koti*
coconut, ripe – *nazi*
coconut, drinking – *dafu*
coffee – *kahawa*
coils, mosquito – *dawa ya mbu ya kuwashia*
cold – *baridi*
comb – *kitana*
come (v) – *kuja*
come here – *njoo hapa*
common, customary – *ya kawaida*
conductor – *kandakta*
cook (v) – *pika*
corn, maize – *mahindi*
cotton – *pamba*
country – *nchi*
crab – *kaa*
craftsman – *fundi*
crocodile – *mamba*
cup – *kikombe*
cut (v) – *kata*

D

dance (v) – *cheza dansa*
danger – *hatari*
date (eg, 12 July) – *tarehe*
daughter, son – *mwana*
day – *siku*
  (for Days of the Week, and Dates, see chapter on Time)

daytime – *mchana*
decide – *kata shauri*
deep – *mto sana*
detergent – *omo/sabuni*
diarrhoea, have (v) – *hara*
die (v) – *kufa*
different – *mbali mbali*
disease – *ugonjwa*
dish, plate – *sahani*
do, make (v) – *fanya*
doctor – *daktari*
done, cooked, ripe – *ya kuiva*
down – *chini*
drink (v) – *nywa*
drive (v) – *endesha*
driver – *dereva*
dry – *kavu*
dysentry, have (v) – *hara damu*

E
each – *kila moja*
eat (v) – *kula*
egg – *yai* (pl: *mayai*)
elder – *mzee*
elephant – *ndovu, tembo*
empty – *tupu*
end – *mwisho*
enough – *ya kutosha, ya kushiba*
enter – *ingia*
especially – *hasa*
every – *kila*
everyone – *kila mtu*

expensive – *ghali*
explain (v) – *eleza*
eye – *jicho* (pl: *macho*)
eyeglasses – *miwani*

F

faeces – *mavi, choo*
farewell – *kwa heri*
farmer – *mkulima*
fat – *mafuta*
father – *baba*
fever – *homa*
fire – *moto*
firewood – *kuni*
first – *ya kwanza*
fish – *samaki*
flowers – *maua*
follow (v) – *fuata*
food – *chakula*
for – *kwa*
forest – *mwituni*
fork – *uma*
freshwater – *maji tamu*
fried – *ya kaanga*
friend – *rafiki* (pl: *marafiki*)
from – *kutoka*
front, in – *mbele ya*
fruit – *matunda*

G

garlic – *vitunguu saumu*
gasoline, petrol – *petroli*

get (v) – *pata*
giraffe – *twiga*
give (v) – *kupa*
glass – *glasi*
go (v) – *kwenda*
  go to sleep – *kwenda kulala*
  go to toilet – *kwenda haja*
goat – *mbuzi*
god – *mungu*
good – *mzuri*
goodbye – *kwa heri*

H

hand – *mkono*
heading (v) – *be elekea*
hear (v) – *sikia*
heat – *joto*
her (object, eg, to her) – *yeye*
her (possessive, eg, her book) – *yake*
here – *hapa*
high – *ya juu*
his – *yake*
home – *nyumbani*
hospital – *hospitali*
hot – *ya moto*
hotel 'lodging' – *hoteli ya kulalia*
hour – *saa*
house – *nyumba*
hurry – *haraka*
husband – *bwana, mume*

I

I – *mimi*
if – *kama*
important – *muhimu*
impossible – *haiwezikani*
in – *katika*
Indian – *mhindi*
infested – *yenye wadudu*
insect – *mdudu* (pl: *wadudu*)
insect spray – *dawa ya wadudu*
inside – *ndani*
instead – *badala ya*
iron – *chuma*
iron (v) – *piga pasi*

J

job – *kazi*

K

kerosene – *mafuta ya taa*
key – *ufunguo, kifunguo*
kind – *aina*
kitchen – *jikoni*
knife – *kisu*
know (v) – *jua*

L

lake – *ziwa*
large – *kubwa*
last – *ya mwisho*
later – *baadaye*
laugh (v) – *cheka*

learn (v) – *jifunza*
leave (v) – *ondoka*
left – *kushoto*
leg – *mguu*
legs – *miguu*
lentils – *dengu*
let's go – *twende*
lie (v) – *sema uwongo*
lights – *taa*
like, if – *kama*
like (v) – *penda*
limes – *ndimu*
lion – *simba*
listen (v) – *sikiliza*
little – *kidogo*
lobster – *kamba*
lodging – *lodjingi*
long – *ndefu*
look (v) – *tazama*
lose (v) – *poteza*
lost, be (v) – *potea*

M

machete, bush knife – *panga*
madam – *bibi, mama*
make (v) – *fanya*
malaria – *homa, malaria*
malaria medicine – *dawa ya malaria*
man – *mwanamume, mtu*
mangoes – *maembe*
many – *nyingi*
marketplace – *sokoni*

me, I – *mimi*
meaning – *maana*
meat – *nyama*
medicine – *dawa*
meet (v) – *onana na*
men – *wanaume, watu*
metal – *chuma*
middle – *kati ya*
milk – *maziwa*
minute – *dakika*
mirror – *kioo*
mister – *bwana*
mixture – *mchanganyiko*
money – *pesa*
more – *zaidi, ingine*
morning – *asubuhi*
mosquitoes – *mbu*
mother – *mama*
mountain – *mlima*
movies, cinema – *sinema*
much – *nyingi*
music – *musiki*
Muslim – *mwisilamu*
must – *lazima*
mutton (goat) – *mbuzi*
  sheep, lamb – *kondoo*
my – *yangu*

N
name – *jina*
need (v) – *hitaji*
needle – *sindano*

never – *kamwe*
new – *mpya*
news – *habari*
night – *usiku*
no – *hapana*
noise – *kelele*
normally – *kwa kawaida*
now – *sasa*

O
ocean – *bahari*
odour – *harufu*
of – *ya*
oil – *mafuta*
on top, over – *juu ya*
one – *moja*
onions – *vitunguu*
opener – *kifunguo*
or – *au*
oranges – *machungwa*
other – *ingine*
our – *yetu*
outside – *nje*

P
packet – *pakiti*
pail – *ndoo*
pants, trousers – *suruali*
papayas – *paipai*
paper – *karatasi*
parrafin (kerosene) – *mafuta ya taa*
parents – *wazazi*

peace – *salama*
people – *watu*
pepper – *pilipili*
perhaps – *labda*
person – *mtu*
photocopy – *fotocopi*
photograph – *picha*
pillow – *mto*
pineapples – *nanasi*
place – *pahali*
plastic – *plastiki, nailon*
police – *polisi*
pork – *nyama ya nguruwe*
porter – *hamali*
potatoes – *vyazi*
prawn – *kamba*
pregnant – *mwenye mimba*
price – *bei*
problem – *matata*
put (v) – *weka*

Q
question – *swali*
quickly – *haraka, upesi upesi*

R
razor – *kijembe*
reduce (v) – *punguza*
remain (v) – *baki*
remember (v) – *kumbuka*
respect – *heshima*
rest (v) – *pumzika*

restaurant – *hoteli ya chakula*
return – *rudi*
rice – *mchele*
right – *kwa kulia*
ripe – *ya kuiva*
river – *mto*
road – *njia*
room – *rumu, chumba*
rotten – *mbovu*
rubber – *mpira*

S

salt – *chumvi*
school – *skuli, shule*
see (v) – *ona*
shark – *papa*
sharp – *kali*
she, he – *yeye*
sheep – *kondoo*
shirt – *shati*
shoes – *viatu*
shop – *duka*
short – *fupi*
shrimp – *kamba*
since, from – *kutoka*
sir – *bwana*
skin – *ngozi*
sleep (v) – *lala*
slowly – *pole pole*
small – *kidogo*
smile – *tabasamu*
snake – *nyoka*

soap – *sabuni*
son, daughter – *mwana*
spaghetti – *spageti, makaronya*
speak (v) – *sema*
spices – *bizari, dawa*
spinach – *mchicha*
start (v) – *anza*
station – *stesheni*
stay – *kaa*
still – *bado*
stop (v) – *simama*
stop – *kituo*
straight – *moja kwa moja*
stranger, guest – *mgeni* (pl: *wageni*)
street – *njia*
student – *mwanafunzi* (pl: *wanafunzi*)
sugar – *sukari*
sweet – *tamu*

T

tailor – *mshoni*
take, carry (v) – *chukua*
taxi – *teksi*
tea – *chai*
teacher – *mwalimu* (pl: *walimu*)
tell (v) – *ambia*
thank you – *asante*
that – *ile*
these – *hizi*
thing – *kitu*
this – *hii*
those – *zile*

thread – *uzi*
ticket – *tikiti*
tinned – *ya mkebe*
together – *pamoja*
toilet – *choo* (pl: *vyoo*)
toilet paper – *karatasi ya choo*
tomato – *nyanya*
tonight – *leo usiku*
too – *pia*
toothbrush – *mswaki*
toothpaste – *dawa ya meno*
towel – *tauli*
town – *mji*
tyre – *mpira*

U
under – *chini ya*
until – *mpaka*
upcountry – *bara*
use (v) – *tumia*

V
vegetables – *mboga*
vehicle – *gari*
very – *sana*
vomit (v) – *tapika*

W
want (v) – *taka*
  (I want to........ – *nataka ku........* + verb)
warm, hot – *ya moto*
wash clothes (v) – *fua*

wash hands (v) – *nawa*
wash self, bathe (v) – *oga*
watch (v) – *tazama*
watch – *saa*
water – *maji*
we, us – *sisi*
week – *wiki*
welcome – *karibu*
what – *nini, gani*
   (for who, when, where, etc, see Interrogative words in
   Grammar chapter)
whole – *mzima*
wife – *mke, bibi*
wind – *upepo*
wine – *mvinyo, wain*
with – *na*
woman – *mwanamke* (pl: *wanawake*)
wood, tree – *mti*
word – *neno*
work – *kazi*

Y

year – *mwaka*
yes – *ndiyo*
yesterday – *jana*
you – *wewe*
young – *kijana*
your – *yako*

Language survival kits

Burmese phrasebook
Speaking Burmese will help you make the most of the limited time you are allowed in Burma. This book contains many useful phrases, complete with Burmese script.

China phrasebook
China's official language, Mandarin (*Putonghua*) is covered in this phrasebook. It includes both conventional *pinyin* spellings and Chinese characters for all phrases.

Hindi/Urdu phrasebook
Hindi is spoken in north India; Urdu is spoken in Pakistan. Both languages are closely related so they have been combined in this doubly useful book.

Indonesia phrasebook
A little Indonesian is easy to learn, and it's almost identical to Malay so this book is doubly useful. The rewards for learning some *Bahasa* are far greater than the effort involved!

Nepal phrasebook
Nepali is spoken in parts of India, Sikkim and Bhutan as well as Nepal. This phrasebook includes a special trekking chapter.

Language survival kits

Papua New Guinea phrasebook
Pidgin is PNG's lingua franca, also spoken with minor variations in the Solomon Islands and Vanuatu. Pidgin will be especially useful in the countryside and on the islands.

Sri Lanka phrasebook
This phrasebook covers Sinhala, the official national language of Sri Lanka. It's an ancient language with a complicated script but its pronunciation is not difficult.

Thailand phrasebook
This phrasebook uses easy-to-follow pronunciation symbols but also includes Thai script. This allows you to 'point and show'.

Tibet phrasebook
Few Tibetans speak English, so it is important to be able to communicate in their language. Tibetan is also spoken in other parts of China, Nepal, Sikkim and Ladakh.